AF415785

First published in 2020 by

Schism press²

First edition
ISBN: 9798667572978

Copyright © Paul Cunningham

Cover image and frontispiece: *Ant* (2020) by Sam Shoemaker

Printed in London, UK.

At home he feels like a tourist
At home he feels like a tourist
He fills his head with culture
He gives himself an ulcer
He fills his head with culture
He gives himself an ulcer

– Gang of Four, "At Home He's a Tourist"

THE HOUSE OF
THE TREE OF SORES

BEDROOM……..3

LIVING ROOM………19

KITCHEN………43

BATH & STORAGE…………57

THE TREE OF SORES……….77

BESKÄRA!

Do not be scared…

BESKÄRA!

Do not, do not be scared…

BESKÄRA!

Cut it out, cut it out…

CUT IT, CUT IT OUT!

Do not, do not cut it…

CUT IT, CUT IT OUT OF YOU!

Cut it out, cut it out…

DO NOT, DO NOT BE SCARED!

BESKÄRA!!!

BE SCARED!!!!!!

BE SCARED!!!

BE SCARED!!!

BEDROOM

But don't worry, honey don't worry
This is just a fairytale
Happening in the supermarket

– The Raincoats, "Fairytale in the Supermarket"

Still awake. I am training myself to lucid dream. I put the special glasses on. There are tiny lights surrounding each lens, timed to go off at a specified time. I wear the tiny lights surrounding each lens. The tiny lights surrounding each lens will blink on-off-on-off at precisely 4 AM. Am I committed to this? I don't know yet. I am trying to commit myself to something. At precisely 4 AM my special glasses will blink like Christmas lights. I am sleeping in the bedroom section tonight. I am sleeping in the bedroom section because the Instruction Manual has instructions. The glasses work best if I sleep on a bed that is not *my* bed. My project requires a *foreign* bed. Luckily, I am sleeping on a bed so foreign that it's called a floor model.

It's supposed to be about *Finding Comfort in Discomfort*. The glasses *should* blink on-off-on-off at 4 AM and I *should* be able to lucid dream. My rooftops will begin blinking and I will be in control. I will be in the bedroom section, but my ceiling won't necessarily have to be a ceiling. If all goes according to plan. If all goes according to plan, my floor won't necessarily have to be a floor. My bedroom section won't have to be a bedroom section if I don't want it to be. Then again, I don't know what I am talking about and I might not know until approximately 4 AM.

My body is lying on a foreign object just as the Instruction Manual recommended. I knew a soldier once who told me all foreign objects are explosive. He was convinced all foreign objects were a threat. He was only 18. He is dead now, but it's okay. I've tried telling myself that. *It's okay*—many, many times. It's difficult to breathe through flag-fabric. A deep breath in a hospital corridor. A face, a violent push against viscose fabric. There is a tag attached. I feel it up against my lips. Fabrication. I feel it. A tag attached.

I am a tag attached. I am without sleep. As an American, I cannot stop thinking about the word: *foreign*. Another soldier once told me that in some foreign films Americans are called *foreigners*. I told him I don't watch the films with the words on the bottom. I don't watch many films at all. Have I mentioned I am the assistant manager of your local IKEA? Have I mentioned your local IKEA is not necessarily so local? Have I mentioned the soldier who was killed by a foreign object? Because I'm not supposed to talk about that at work. He was only 18. I can hear my boss. He's somewhere off screen making an on-off-on-off sound with his eyes.

On-off-on-off. I can only see my hands and I'm crawling on the floor. I feel awake and the floor feels cold. I'm not sure if I like this feeling. Being awake and being asleep. My fingernails feel like they're digging. Digging a little into the floor. The floor feels gypsum-delicate. The floor feels hollow when I knock my weight around it. I feel like I'm a third-grader again playing a third-grade recess game we used to play. *Stand on my chest*, someone would say in a strong-sounding voice. Third-graders taking turns standing on the strongest third-grader's chest. Playground. Painful sounds. I'm going to fall through the floor any second now. There are metallic holes in this floor. Suddenly, I pass something that looks like it belongs on a ceiling. On-off-on-off.

Still awake. I think about the *awake* word and I find myself staring up at the ceiling in the bedroom section. I reach into my pocket and feel for my keys. Still there. I'm still the assistant manager of the local IKEA. I'm glad none of my co-workers know I've been spending my nights here. I *hope* none of my co-workers know I've been spending my nights here. The bedroom section contains bedroom objects. The bedroom section contains a fake bedroom door. The bedroom section contains a knock-knock-knock from the same bedroom door. Is that me knocking? Am I giving up tonight? Only a knock-knock-knock at the same fake front door. *Hello there, I'm an assistant manager. You must be looking for something. You must be interested in a piece of furniture, right? Are you a door-to-door? Are you a salesman? Just a man? What's that? You'd like to know what IKEA means in Swedish?* From where I stand, the fake front door looks very real. From where I stand, I feel the pulse of another on-off-on-off.

There's a lot of room for my arms in these rooms. *Are you an American,* whispers the bedroom section. *Yes,* I say. *What do you dream of,* whispers the bedroom section. *They've not been good dreams lately*, I say. *I've been trying to find the Comfort in Discomfort and my dreams have not been good ones lately.* Again, a knock-knock-knock at the door. *Does all that knocking make you feel uncomfortable,* whispers the bedroom section. *Well, yes. I suppose that it does. It does make me feel uncomfortable.* There's just no peace in this bedroom section. I could really use some living room right now. Again, a knock-knock-knock at the door. *Why not just answer the door,* whispers the bedroom section. *Because,* I say. *I don't speak Swedish. I cannot translate it.*

You'd still like to know what IKEA means in Swedish? From where I stand, the fake front door looks very real. I must send it something. I decide I will fake-translate. I will send electricity up the side of the fake front door and deliver a shock, I shall make something up: *The word is actually an acronym for . . .* I stop and I stammer. I wish this long knock-around would come to a close. *With all due respect, the company started in Sweden, not America. Swedish trivia is not part of my job description.* They nod. I nod. They nod. I nod. They understand. *We understand,* they say. I understand. They go on their way. I close my eyes and I relax into my surrounding furniture. Well-furnished lies.

My keys jingle. They remind me that I am an authority figure. After all, I am still managing my night. After all, I am a keyhole kind of guy. I am a keyhole kind of guy and there's a lot of door in this bedroom. There's a lot of sale potential. There's a lot of stilt. I'm a stiltwalker, you see. I'm a walker on stilts in this 4 AM space. The stilts are for doing inventory. How can I properly do inventory if I can't reach everything? Nothing must be out of reach. I reach for a children's toy, a pink plush pig. Suddenly, I notice the soft plush pig has nipples and I get angry. Why do the Swedes want their children to play with nippled pigs? *I've not had good dreams lately*, I tell the soft plush nippled pig. *I've been trying to find the Comfort in Discomfort and they've not been good ones lately*. I pledge allegiance. *Where does your allegiance lie*, whispers the soft plush pig. I pledge. I pledge, like a boy under stars and stripes. Flag-fabric and toe tags. On-off-on-off.

Here, the rice paper floor lamp sways. Here, the fake front door repeatedly offers new limbs. Limbs tagged to customer-bodies. Limbs, Ziploc-bagged for clean handshakes. Clean, clean customers, or no customers at all. Incoming: customers with their wide canvas bodies. Late night customers, what languages are they? Am I dreaming them? *I'm sorry, we're closed*, I say. That's when I notice their little bleed-through lines. Barcodes form on their canvas bodies. Something is coming out of them. Something is seeping onto the floor I am expected to manage. I am expected to mop, I am expected to keep everything clean. *What have you swallowed? What have you eaten?* They look at one another and then they look at me. They smell like American cleaning products. *Our sores are getting heavy.* The night becomes banana-rot spotted. I can't have the other Americans smudging this authentic Swedish interior.

Will there be evening party parlor amusements, they ask. I lose my patience. I scream . I tear the flesh from their bodies. I tear their rice paper away. Wire frames stand cold. Dawn's early light. To my surprise, only floor lamps sway. No living, breathing bodies inside the store. *Oh, I thought you were foreigners, but I must be dreaming.* I stare at the floor lamps. *Foreigner is another word for immigrant, right? Or is immigrant the preferred term?* The lamps do not answer. I stare at the fake front door and again there comes a knock-knock-knock. Ajar, the fake front door. Paint flakes fly out on the gust of a whisper: *Will there be evening party parlor amusements or not?* I thought I heard something, and it felt like that something was inching its way inside me. It felt like a tree branch. A tentacle. A reverse-umbilical cord. Something entering my bellybutton . . . On-off-on-off.

Who's there? Is that a Stockholm sofa? A Stockholm 2-drawer? A Stockholm 5? Adjustable arms, a space to thrive. Much-needed floor space, a much needed "MORE" space. A stranger's voice asks many questions: *Are you interested in a game of Hot Cockles? What about a bit of Shadow Buff? Maybe a round of Stagecoach or two?* (Bang! Bang!) The stranger enters the bedroom section through the fake bedroom door. Things feel like they aren't so fake anymore. *No Stagecoaching, please*, I plead. *What makes you think this is a western?* Something whispers, something else cackles. Easy-gliding and self-closing, the furniture sets me up to play the right tune. *Tale as old as time.* I'm a music box with a folding bin lid. Battery operated. Conductor sold separately. Hear that? Something growling like a timpani. *Dom. Död. Död. Död. Dom. Död. Död. Död. Dom. Död. Död. Död. Dom.*

4 AM, I am. I am scared of this number: four. I have uttered the four letters for as long as I can remember. 1 AM. 2 AM. 3 AM. 4 AM. *Ante meridiem.* Latin for "before midday" and next thing you know: dinner is served! Middag! Something is digging its way into my hollow scar, my twisted navel. My umbilical ring, it is hard as stone. *Dom. Dröm. Dröm. Dröm.* My stomach feels fuller, intra-abdominal pressure. Fuller with future. *Din framtidsdröm är ett shopping schema,* something whispers. *Your future dream is a shopping scheme,* something whispers. Four as long as I can remember: *Dom. Dröm. Dröm. Dröm.*

LIVING ROOM

There's too many closets

– Sex Pistols, "Holidays in the Sun"

On-off-on-off. Am I dreaming or is this furniture funhousing me? My voice or their voice? One voice or voices? Living bodies? Living rooms? Machine-woven? I must be funhoused. Everything is labeled around here. Labels with label holders. Stockholm coffee table, Stockholm glass-door cabinet, Stockholm chandelier. Is this Stockholm? With latex backing? With foil finish? Is this Stockholm? Box stackable, box stockable. Scenic, made from recycled paper.

I, I—

      how it turns into a bed at night.

                I, I—

Är hem där hjärtat är?

Sjukdom goes the drum, hålheartedly. *Sjukdom, dom, dom, dom.* Blood dragged and dragning. *Dom, dröm, dom dröm.* Hålheartedly, hullhearted all hårt the heartgel orgel, the *pump-pump* all blixt-blistered. Hårt-hearted, this evening blod-dröm. No good blod, no gud good. I'm all dödblod, yeah? Dådblod, yeah? Dad's blood drums against the dollartechnet bottom. Mörka-mobile, långsamt. I'm just another long shot. I'm the night's drum. The dröms drum. The *dom, död*. The *död, dom*. The doldrums. The oerhort odd and always hurting. Never the right rytm.

Hur har din släkthistoria bestämt din kultur

Kill, killing, killed country. Muskeln country. Kiln country, clay country leering lera röd country. It's not my fält country of expertise country. Fält of experience cuntry bubblade bryter, bryter, bryter country. Bride her country. Paternal perterna person pressure. Can't take it. Can't take it any lungor. Gore gör gore. Syrsor sounds cutting through the family rötter. Betong tree fodder. Bebodd photo album, feberning möbler. Man or woman language rötter? Take a foreign language test. Determine your proficiency. Kiss the kock. Can this living room astroturf support all kultur kreatur?

Hur växer din trädgård?

With silverbells and cockleshells? Have you considered enchanced beauty? You can't live in a room without artificial flora. Fejka flora. Fake fejka and potted fejka. Fejka green and fejka vines, and no dead leaves on the floor. No dead leaves to sweep, only *dröm, dröm, dröm* on the floor. Fake, fejka faces on the floor of your gården. *En grön tanke i en grön nyans,* something whispers. Something whispers a carpet of grön, a groaning room of green grounds, of walls of green gröning. Silver vingar spread across the room, reflecting no smila. Silver vingar spread.

Vilka typer av historien är viktigast i din identitet?

Faglarna mönster, Hitchcock krökta. Bryter birds, raid glittrade. Kiss the kock. Kiss him, bro. Kiss him. Did you kiss him? Fag larynx! Tar slut! No future! The violent birds fly out when nu kultur opens its mouth. Gymnasium noises. Oral exams. Olja exams. All your exams. Tanning sessions. Brodorangea squeals with his dumbbells. Brodorangea grunts his mönster language. He is not foreign. He could never be foreign. He was born in America. Him. Gymnasium noises. Hymns. Sucked off. Hemsökt av. Röd, white, and blue. No homo.

Man eller kvinna?

Hush hush, little babe, hush us husgrundground abs and abs and drawers and drawers of abs and absbladder every roomful every last bullfull fully garlanded, bloodblood rains from taurobolium ground roars and roars och rör! Cushion abs all sofa all so fab abs of stainless steel-through still under grundbeef all bull all the time of husband husgrund all histrionics all a basis beefing. Tin Man. Abs-Man, absing all wall-mounted absing all abysmal. Honest Abesman, Gatorade-emblazoned with adjustable arms protruding forward, forward, forward (THIRSTY) March, deposits (STILL THIRSTY) April, deposits (BLOODTHIRSTY) May, deposits these months deposit stuntman after stuntman (SOIL-RESISTANT PUBLICITY STUNTS) one after another. High-def stuntmen and bulk-up dead lifts, all jackhammering about. Nothing sterling, nothing sterile. Interior, bakterier. Moth-eaten, closet-scented. Closed, I'm sorry we're just too far closed off. Lad not out. Sad, sad lad. Outvecklade? House. White House. House. White House. House, high-def clean-and-press reps keep up the up and up keeps well-maintained those water-retaining muscles. One-aim, dumbbell up down like a hot bod bebodd eftersom school games of Tooth for a Tooth, maybe Eye for an Eye? Lilla American Country, where gentleman has so much to show for his ingen eftersom handling, eftersom grabbing, eftersom real rad muterad Mustanging, must strangle 'em eftersom bullblood, eftersom pungsackar superior. Bakterier.

**Finns det en avgift för montering av möbler
vid leverans?**

Produktiv, television producer Hollywood producer of glitz and
glimtar. Money sak reproduceras as as fast as pansarglas.
Bullet-proof glass. Lilla holes from lilla bullets. Lilla röd stains.
Siren-saturated night. Oversaturated. Översättning. *The fog is
too thick here.* We need more ground-up foreign materials,
more husgrund materials. More mörk materia. Aase Bergssidor.
Not all this nylon frame, erectile tissue of Fifth Avenue.
Centimeters by centimeters by centimeters by centimeters.
Hjälp, hjälp! 9-1-1, I need a känslor counselor. *No, you need to
be monitored.* Gentlemen, start your sondmatar. *Some assembly
required.* (Can be employed to further employ camera shake.)
Noun, linking verb, predicate adjective. (Waterproof and
fogproof.) *Noun, verb.* (Designed for photographers and
graphic designers.) *Noun, intransitive verb.* Untranslatable
verve. (Blades provide excellent blurring effects to out-of-focus
areas.) *Noun, verb, direct object.* (On a computer or mobile
device, you can shift the living picture in any direction.) *When
the time is up, the player reads his or her sentences aloud.
Other players can challenge the player if they think the verb
tense is wrong.* (Continuous shooting.) *The team that has more
points at the end of the game wins.* (Continuous shooting.) *It's
all about winning.* (Continuous shooting.)

Vad   värdesätter   du?

Trädet, you bet. Must be familiar with the familj. The hushåll, the hush-hall. Now hush! If you understand, just nod. Just nod. Andnöd. No laughing. No lafsiga slafs. Vad värdesätter du? Your own tree-leak? Your own sap-sak? You sad sak! Trädet traitor? Having a weak lungor sak week? Hickory or oåkt? Just a lilla joke. Ro, ro, ro your warship! Gently down your wirelessly streamed content. Underage heterosexual femporn? There's a femton. That's my boy, that's my son. Slums and porn. Slamporna torpor. Dekorativa. Divas. Jämn jam spread on man hands. Masturbating for money, those silverfläckar. Familjoke. Familjarring. Familjacking. Cold cake frosten. Crime scene systrar. SVU cyst stars. Chaturbating, hemsökt. Befolkning bebodda.

Hör du det?

تحـــذير _ AMARA _ PERINGATAN _ UWAGA _ 경고 _ UYARI _

_ UPOZORENJE! _ OPOZORILO _ ACHTUNG _ UPOZORNENIE _ ATENŢIE! _

_ ΠΡΟΕΙΔΟΠΟΙΗΣΗ _ ВНИМАНИЕ _ IMPORTANTE _ UPOZORENJE _ ĮSPĖJIMAS _

_ WARNING _ 警告 _ FIGYELEM _ AVVERTENZA _ VAROVÁNÍ _ VAROITUS _

_ VIÐVÖRUN _ WAARSCHUWING _ ADVARSEL _ AVERTISSEMENT _

V A R N I N G

Kan du rekommendera en exterminator?

He-man, peppered, salted. Young ones. Fanged ones. Fånga och släpp? A game or two? *No slapping.* Not just a slap or two. *A slap isn't good enough.* What harm ever came from a release-ending game? Something more lethal. Need them a gift for their gabbing. Need them their rat-a-tat-tat, those råttor. We need to wreck those thick-tailed insects. Insektsmedel, those meddling ones. Tiny meddling ones. Need to leave 'em gegging on my klibbig. Clinging for life, pitfälla after pitfälla. Must fail, they must. Mustfälla. Fälla after fälla. Well-svälted meat fälla, those fellas. Krävning cravings. Toxisk risk, manipulated spinal discs. Rigged ryggmärg. A wholesale must-fail. Mustfälla. Down on their luktfri. Luxury B-B-Q, you don't eat for free. Snabbverkande, feeling snob-toxic. Legs flailing. A wholesale must-fail. Prisoner legs. Sounds like a syrsors sax. Sounds like rats on their backs. Gagging, gegging. Thank you for your patronage.

Vad är din retur politik?

Truth your mouth for 30 days used your mouth for 30 days
truth now for 30 days your money chewed back, no time. Your
30 days guarantees kvävning, your 30 days guarantees
deydrering, your 30 days guarantees svält, now solve for y.
*Have you not completed your foreign language test? How many
firecrackers do you own?* There's no waking Uncle Sömn
without the right gift. Be proud, be loud. Invade other
territories. 30 days, no kemisk risks, no need to leave lickety-
split. A truck passes you, somebody spits. Subtitles are un-
American.

I'm bod stackable, bod stalkable. I'm sitting down to protect my contents. To protect my content. And this floor model sofa I've slept on? Am sitting on? Am slept on? Suitable for any space? Removable cushions. *Tear me apart. Use your fingers.* Contoured, empty. Too many voices. Horizontal springs. Woven strings. Hallway noise, a puddle splash. Horizontal, vertical. Horizontical. Armchair voices, armchair greyness. What exactly makes an arm chair? Horticulture. Living room jacuzzi limbs? Max load ___ lbs. That's a lot of lbs. A lot of limbs. A lot of mad-libbing in the living room. Look at the Malmö wallpaper. Sense those meatball scents. Am I in Malmö? A house in Malmö? A lived-in house? A played-in house? A prayed-in house? A house of screams. *Where has the light gone? Where has the light gone?*

Off-off-off-off. But I hope to live inside this furniture the way a hand lives inside a puppet. Temporarily. Things aren't going how they should be going. Something feels off. How this one living room resembles many rooms for living. Varying motifs for living. How low the sunlight in this windowless living room section. How gone my space seams. I need to get out of this living room section, but I feel like I'm only crawling in circles. I feel like I've been here before. This wasn't what the dream was supposed to be. There were supposed to be pretty lights like Christmas and pretty snow like Hollywood. But here I sit dreaming on a foreign sofa among dozens of other foreign sofas. The sofas have mouths like in a cartoon. But they're not saying what I want them to say and there's too many of them. They don't understand. They haven't read the Instruction Manual. It said *I* should feel comfortable.

It's about Finding Comfort in Discomfort, whispers my foreign bed. My floor model sofa. It lips me up as it opens wide. It cushions up-down and sneezes lint. Its breath reeks of organophosphates. Its body appears to have absorbed a fair share of insecticides. Pesticides. Homicides and matricides. My mattress sides, they ache. My nervous system feels a bit off. Am I still an authority? I can't decide. *Tell me about your ideal home.* Again, the sofa's whispers stain: *Will it make the same impression you try to make with your clothing? With your uniform? With your heavy cologne? With your cufflinks and your ties? With the people you know? Is it you? Does it smell like you? Does it sound like you? Do you think I sound like you? Will your open house welcome families? What about children? Will you share their non-consenting bodies in a Facebook news feed?* I walk away from the soft-whispering sofa. I pass empty seat after empty seat. Side-by-sides and in-betweens. I imagine bodies sitting, hand-in-hand. The finest in national programming. I trail off to a mattress pile stacked to the ceiling. A post-inventory pile-up. A trunk of stains. A tree of sores.

The swelling mattress sides burst open, pushing milky leaves from their coiling insides. Rusty springs and tangles of chicken wire. One mattress pukes out a little girl covered in steaming leaves. Another mattress grunts out a little boy covered in soil and wiggling maggots. My nervous system aches. The little girl runs over to a fake living room containing lots of pillows and stripes. The little boy runs over to a fake living room containing many paper lamps and fake plants. Each child tears a transparent curtain from the fake window of their respective living room. Each child wraps their transparent curtain piece around their head. Twist, twist. Over their mouths, over their eyes. Twist, twist. They quickly join one another inside a fake living room containing a fireplace. *Every family needs a good—* Twist, twist. Together, they jump up and down on a sofa. *Kan du se mig? Kan du se mig?* they scream. But this isn't the family I should have. The dream is all wrong. Is someone screaming? Hear that? They can't even scream in English. How embarrassing! So I'm not going to answer. I turn my back on them and they turn a television on. The off-off-off-off feels darker and darker.

The television's torrent flows into the children for hours. *My throat feels dry*, it finally whispers. It shuts itself off. The foreign children build a fire in the fireplace of the fake living room. They wait until it gets nice and big. They wait until it is network prime time big. They leap into the fire and have themselves a pretend telephone conversation. The burning little girl asks, *Kan you sig me now?* The burning little boy holds his fist to his ear and answers, *Sorry, our public relations department has been working with government bureaus to monitor legislation and political activities of interest to our business. Thank you for your patience.* The burning little girl holds her fist to her ear and cries, *DU SER ME?*

The burning little boy answers, *Sorry, I am currently evaluating and administering and developing and devising and determining and advancing and estimating and proofreading and representing and substituting and promoting and explaining and assisting and proceeding.* Some flesh melts from the burning little girl's lower jaw. *Wait, I want you to give me a chance. No more Svenska*, she cries. *That's the ticket*, says the little boy. *Now you're speaking my language.* Some of the flesh melts from the burning little boy's cheeks. Somewhere a floor model sofa is whisper-singing, *Youuuuu are sixteen going on seventeen…*

You are seventeen going on eighteen. I'll depend on youuuuuu… Are they teasing me because I am the assistant manager? They must think I'll take control of their excess, their messy limbs. They must know I'm an American. Have I mentioned the soldier who was killed by the foreign object? He stepped on a foreign object in a desert and his body exploded. Now he's buried under that swollen tree of sores. That family tree of rifles and ammunition. He was 18 years old. Just a boy. We went to high school together. *He wasn't a boy,* something whispers. *He was a man. He was a man who died for his country. You should be proud of him.*

Bring our solider home, something whispers. *Stay out of my home,* something whispers. *In the interest of public safety,* something whispers. *They don't talk like us,* something whispers. *Believe in what I believe in,* something whispers. *He might have been a deserter,* something whispers. *Why are you supporting that deserter,* something whispers. *This room needs more shelves,* something whispers. *This wall needs more frames,* something whispers. *Police line—do not cross,* something whispers. *Why don't you believe me,* something whispers. *We tortured no one,* something whispers. *I've almost finished the screenplay,* something whispers. *Go back to where you came from,* something whispers. *And the Oscar goes to,* something whispers. *Give 'em the death penalty,* something whispers. *Dom. Död. Död. Död. Dom. Död. Död. Död*

I should have told the boy-soldier that I loved him when I had the chance. I was afraid to, I was afraid to. He is dead now, a man now. Gone. *Sjukdom* goes the drum, hålheartedly. *Sjukdom, dom, dom, dom.* Blood dragged and dragning. *Dom, dröm, dom dröm.* Hålheartedly, hullhearted all hårt the heartgel orgel, the *pump-pump* all blixt-blistered. Hårt-hearted, this evening blod-dröm. No good blod, no gud good. I'm all dödblod, yeah? Dådblod, yeah? Dad's blood drums against the dollartechnet bottom. Mörka-mobile, långsamt. I'm just another long shot. I'm the night's drum. The dröms drum. The *dom, död.* The *död, dom.* The doldrums. The oerhort odd and always hurting. Never the right rytm.

"A tree of sores." A reference to a painting by David Lynch called, "Suddenly My House Became a Tree of Sores" (1990). When asked about his film *Eraserhead* (1997) Lynch has said, "If it's from my own life, I don't see it. It's from so far inside, hidden, that it can only come out in an idea, which kind of balloons out. I don't know where it comes from. My childhood was picket fences, blue skies, red flowers, and cherry trees— but then I would see millions of little ants swarming on the cherry tree, which had pitch oozing out of it. I noticed these little things but mostly what I saw was very happy. It was good times on our street—that's my life. When I first saw New York and Philadelphia, they made a huge impression on me because the contrast was so great. It hit me harder. I really saw it, and I really felt it—the fear was so great it was unbelievable. The things I saw were so foreign, it was like being in another world."

"One mattress pukes out a little girl covered in steaming leaf clumps. Another mattress grunts out a little boy covered in soil and curling maggots. My nervous system aches." Between 2013 and 2014, thousands of people of Roma descent fled to Sweden after the European Union ended restrictions on free movement with Bulgaria and Romania. This resulted in vast numbers of homeless children springing up in various major cities of Sweden.

KITCHEN

Intrusion on personal space
Unlike an animal I jump away
Respect the imaginary circle I draw
Feel it, can you see a false space enhancing?

– The Slits, "Animal Space"

My little chicks are peeping. *The oerhort odd and always hurting*, they peep. *Never the right rytm*, they peep. They are famished. They are family? What should I cook for my fejka flora, my fake children? *Mjölk, mjölk*, they peep and they cry. I shrug away from them, but they follow. *Milk*, I ask. The little boy points to a soft toy cow. The little girl picks up the soft toy cow and throws it at my head. *Let's go look for a kitchen*, I say.

RYTM RECEPT CALLS FOR:

1 work surface
¼ teaspoon brass screws
1 20 ounce can of hex bolts
¼ cup freshly grated grub finials

3 grinds of clear plastic bumpers
½ pound of drywall screws
10 slats twin / full
Churn until thick!

wacky stax eyes on your tarred n' feathered
whisk pretty good together
Swedish Chef selects one plump clucker
and the feathers go flying!
Hinka dinka dergen!
and out out springs mockmjölk

More boomashootns, cry the hands of
puppetland, a microwave-safe home
to dreams and appliances

puppetstringchoked sinkhole
sings a green song a salad-mean song
veggie smiles and stringy ooze
the mockmjölk bubbles

Brush a grill gate with spring tension adjuster
Add 20 #7 x 7/8" flat-head screws
Add ¾ cup of decorative bolts
Use a slotted spoon to mix
Preheat oven to 375' F

In the kitchen: formulaic plots are cooked up
as the hand inside the Swedish Chef
makes a body trip and spill
causes kropps to flood
cue laugh track

Pour batter into prepared bowl!

a bowl is a shed is a shedding
is a clean shed or a shed of fakes?
a should snusk a snusk shed?
identisk, the translation risk

translation, needle in a höstack
a whole stack, a sales rack
a hate-stack, bombar dem
bombard them, feja or fejka?

melon, knocksharps the skull
kitchen offers a mallet, a gavel, a kavel
dough-rolling a skulle, dough-rolling a should
feja skola och fejka skola?

translation, a fruit contains a secret mjölk
behind the peel, *inte gråta över spilld mjölk?*
peel-removal; glöd-core; våld-core
suga sockret, suger socker

orange skin, apelsin
clay-grade translation buggy contains:
many fruits, many skins
kokos, vindruvor, lök, tomat

smiling coconuts, grapes, onions, tomatoes
too many cabbage heads turning
Chop! Chop! Chop!
Swedish Chef begins chopping
Chop! Chop! Chockskadad!

If someone cracks open the hard fruit,
will the wound remain open?

SHED LEAVE THE DOOR UNLOCKED?
SHED THROW AWAY THE KEY?

Shed repeat after me, says Swedish Chef
Jag ska hjälpa den federala polisen!
Live-handing in that antron fleece:
American hand, en röd flagga

Keep your gardin closed, cries puppetland
SLUTSCENEN, translators are stage-whores
canonical storage wars, en härskri!
SLUTSHAMEN TAR, MILITÄR!

NOTES ON THE TEXT

"*Shed repeat after me*, says Swedish Chef puppet." The Swedish Chef Muppet puppet was created by Jim Henson and first appeared on American television in 1975. During the introduction of episode 102 of *The Muppet Show*, Brian Henson said of his father Jim Henson, "[…] he had this tape that he used to play which was 'How to Speak Mock Swedish'. And he used to drive to work and I used to ride with him a lot. And he would drive to work trying to make a chicken sandwich in Mock Swedish or make a turkey casserole in Mock Swedish. It was the most ridiculous thing you had ever seen. And people at traffic lights used to stop and sort of look at him a little crazy. But that was the roots of the character that would eventually become the Swedish Chef. And if you watch the Swedish Chef one of the most exciting things about it is the head is just speaking away and trying to follow the hands which are grabbing meat cleavers and throwing chickens over his head. To me the best part about the Swedish Chef is the more you don't understand him, the more you love him."

"If someone cracks open the hard fruit, / will the wound remain open?" In her book of essays on poetry, *Tsunami from Solaris* (2020), author Aase Berg writes, "Scars can fuse and close holes, including both 'negative' holes (such as wounds) and 'positive' holes (such as the holes needed for nutritional intake). One can consider fossils an extreme form of scar, as well as mold: mold is what happens to food dishes that try to heal and 'grow shut' over a long period of time."

BATH AND STORAGE

The kids in the halls and the pipes in the walls
Make me noises for company
Long distance callers make long distance calls
And the silence makes me lonely

-The Clash, "Lost in the Supermarket"

a *should*

a shed

for more

bodies

I don't feel like a manager anymore. All this cooking makes me feel like a father. My *fejka* children consume until they explode, until they catch fire. I lead the burning little girl and the burning little boy through the store. My little *loggar*. Their fiery hands let go of my gaze and they tip over a nearby shopping cart. I take them by the flames again, I steer them through fake room after fake room until I locate a fake bathroom. The pipes inside produce water. (Oh! This must be a *real* bathroom.) I draw the children a bath, they push out their faces. I put out their fires. *Geg mig kraken*, squeals the boy. *Give you what?* I ask. *Nej, nej! Geg MIG kraken*, squeals the little girl. *A kraken? Octopus?* I ask. The little girl points to something on a shelf behind me. Plush tentacles and soft suckers. I pick it up, study it, show it to them. *Kraken?* They both nod.

But I didn't know we sold crochet kraken, I say. *Where did this come from?* The children ignore my question and splash waves of water from out of their tub. *Stop that*, I yell. The little boy continues splashing; the little girl drums her hands against the side of the tub. *Dröm, dröm, dröm, dröm*, the little girl laughs. *No drum*, I yell back. *No more drum.* I angrily toss the crochet kraken to the floor. *Mardröm?* the little girl laughs. *Mardröm*, the little boy repeats. *Mardröm*, they both giggle. They pull the plug from their tub valve, they watch the water swirl down, down. Suddenly, something hisses from the hole. Bowel vowels. *Mor kraken*, they scream. They leap out of the tub and take to my legs. They hold on tightly, for dear life. *Kissssssta*, the tub hisses. *Kissssssta, kissssssta.*

Synkoperated shots of black slop bust from out of the drainpipe. *Pinka, pinka lilla stjärna*, sings the darkness of the drainpipe. The children choke back tears. The drainpipe gags up a cloacal call, a glowing yellow bubbles out, combines with the black tub-slop. Fattar, fattar—a bläckfisk tentakel. The tentakel protrudes from the tub-sken, unwinds like a spindel. Spits long bleka webs, spreads like the bleakest fog. Spreads across our bodies, spreads across our faces. Bleka sken, blekansikten. Mardröm. Mor, mor. Sinister sex surr(s)ound. A fog of sex, meningslöst sex? The tub sewage flows over the sides. The tentakel whips violently. A coprophagous cornucopia. *Kroppsssspråk*, the tentakel hisses.

Tentakel splits and. Tentakel spits och. Tentakel hardens, carves into the room with axe nerveux. Its goes soft, suddenly spools far off into a corner of the ceiling. Tentakel into the ceiling, the tile lifts away from the ceiling. Glands and palps sprout from each kraken suction cup, long strands of nerve fibers protrude from each tentakel. Swelling with axoplasm, the strands harden into long knots of, long lobes of, long lips of magnocellular bark. *Kraken eller träd?* asks the little boy. *I don't know*, I say. We quickly leave the bathroom as the massive tentakler twist up through the ceiling and into the second floor.

The children follow me onto the escalator. *Mor, mor?* they ask. *More what?* I reply. *Are we going to go look for mother?* the little boy suddenly asks in English. *No, I don't know your mother*, I say. *You married her, pappa*, the little girl replies. *You have me confused with somebody else*, I say. *No we don't pappa.* I ignore their high-pitch; I travel through fake room after fake room looking for the ascending tentakel. *But I suit any space*, the little boy whines. *But I consume up to 30% less energy*, the little girl squeals. *But I'm made from recycled paper,* the little boy whines. *But I have a folding bin-lid,* the little girl squeals.

I find a hole, a wound in the flooring. A dark tree trunk swells. Capillary vessels chafing and spewing their inners from the jagged hole, the shattered floor, slightly shredded pedal arteries still pumping. Charisma, a tree. A chiasma of nerve bundles, branches, dryck lingon-dripping branches and blooming pustules. Neuronal cytoplasm leaks from numerous growth wounds. Weak contractions, respiratory rhythms. Deflated alveoli sway, scabbed-over sections of rough bark. The coiling tree branches continuously, generates muscle. Throbbing grubs. The tree of sores possesses a stomach, the tree of sores possesses an esophagus. I stare at its tongue-like lobes of bark, I stare at its tiny, grinding teeth. Like little motors. I wait for the mouth, for the möter sounds. I wait, I listen as mor sores slowly form.

I wait in the house of the tree of sores. The height-adjustable house of the tree of sores. I wait for its möter to start, for its many teeth to grind. I wade in the mosh pit of household objects, the mosh pit of grotesque möter skills. I spot a commercial proposition drooling in the corner of yet another fake room. My eyes, mutilated by household objects. Ögon. All gone. I can't see straight, I can't—only flickering lights, my suddenly failing eyes. On-Off-On-Off. I stage-dive, I head-bang. On-Off-On-Off. I can't remember my name. I can't remember my name, but I remember the names of my children. *My children? What children?* On-Off-On-Off.

I stand before a trunk of stains, a tree of sores. It quakes and it quakes, it makes mor möter sounds: *Look at yourself, head-banger, why do you stand there, shivering, slurring coldly with your stupid flesh? Why are you neglecting your children? Why are you neglecting their eggs?* The tree of sores quakes once more, spits a crochet kraken from its bark. I pick up the slimy crochet kraken, drenched in child-killing bacteria. I shoot the sharp-jawed tree a punkish grin. *Eggs?* I ask. *They're lost and miming,* the tree answers. *Pecking and performing the everyday gestures of this pop milieu, their pop's mildew. Careful, crash-dummy! Easy, head-banger! You might crash and burn!* My body oddly—it bursts into flames, I drop the crochet kraken to the floor. I stop, drop, and roll. Hundreds of bumps crack loudly beneath my flaming roll. Ägg, ägg, ägg äggulor! ägg, ägg, ägg om, om, omelette, umm, umm, umlaut, a lot, a lot knocking, knocking, knäckt, cracking up. Cracking me up, I cry out.

I dream of forests and the forests turn into nightmares. Nighttime fires across the world. I feel the bark of the tree of sores moaning, howling across min face. Region after region of fire. Ingen vacker trädgård. No life, no liv. I am unsure of my future. Djur borta, upp i rök. Smoking kontinents, smoldering futures. Upp in smoke, this våldvärld. Upp och ner, we have our ups and downs. Outforskat territorium, deliberate terrorism. Bolsonaro dreams of a clean world, dreams of smoke. I see myself in a mirror, smoke. Koala carcasses and no echo. Only wildfires and prisons of people. Prisons of people, prisons of people as far as the eye can see.

Oscar Wilde's last words tried to change his wallpaper. Smoke and mirrors. I part my lips, strike a match, hope for a small explosion. Anything to change the wallpaper. Dandelions have gone to seed. I have no desire to be clean. Somehow, I will push up and I will open, I will bloom into polygala, polyglot. I will grow to shelter the body of a fallen soldier, half-formed leaflets.

Burnt bread, my bread body. Brödkavle, I keep rolling, I roll out my fires. I roll out of my bed. I stare up at the tree, I stare up at the sores. I feel like a bruised roosthole, a local valve, a horahole, a horrorshow. I am up all night, blood flowing. A horhus, a hönshus. Am I hönhus? Hönsnät? Swells of my hen rolled away in the fire, I feel happy about this. *But where are my children? Am I mor? Am I mother? Am I father?* The lateral teeth of the tree clamp down onto my legs, sweeps my body inward. *Are you their mother? Their mother tongue? Am I their mother?* I ask. A channel of tied-together trash bags flap up and surround the fibrous trunk of the tree of sores. Lumen, vesicles of lens-generating tissue fills in. All over, all over. Makes, makes eyes. Eyes of light protrude from the trash bag channel of the tree of sores. Bags of swollen, of shit, of crud. I am up all night, blood flowing. I am swollen, I am shit, I am crud. I am mangled, cranium through a kaffe table book's table of malcontents.

Beak-first, a blue chicken emerges from the trash bag darkness. (My hand-drawn, henjawn little boy.) A yellow chicken emerges from the trash bag darkness. (My hand-drawn, henjawn little girl.) They are my cultish acolytes worn like clipped images, so BAZAAR!, cult prophets snarling, pecking, pipping. They are my children, they are my chickens. Egg-droppers, their assault on my language. I decide to embrace this bellicose, these ventricose vows. I am ignited by translation aorta, blood system. Blood flows through my swollen caruncles, this future crinkled page of lobe.

My many eggs, embedded in the sore-house. My yolkish needs, gnidas. I check the recept, I study my feathered children in this well-furnished bunke bunker. Their blue and yellow colors make them look less American. I didn't want that, I wanted them to develop via bra vibrationer. I take a moment to try and remember my daughter's features, my daughter's name. Was she Kikki or Sanna? I cannot remember, but I remember her holding a microphone. Does she get that from me? Does she have mor of my mor looks or mor of my far looks? What about my son? He looked like a famous Swedish chef, didn't he? Was he Magnus? Didn't he have a hunting dog? Named Krut or Crud? Clearly I cannot recall my little tree, my kvitto tree, my ancient ek, my traditional ick, my family tree, my bra vibrationer. I feel I have been feathered, tarred, censored. These yellows and blues, these new bruise colors. This doesn't feel like the American Dream. *America is however I feel. Right.* It is only a feeling. *It is about finding comfort in discomfort. Right.*

Guitar riffs, death riffs. What am I, gångkläder? *Jag är en fattig översättare!* What am I saying? Shiny leathered, tarred and not feathered. *Pappa, you are lost in translation*, my children giggle. My cranial jelly shakes around in the riot traffic, I mosh into the shit of public decency. I think of chickens, their lilla eggs, their kokning bodies. The strangeness of their foreign language: stjärnor, ränder. Blah, blah. Amerikanerna, kernels popping. Hollywood games of whitewashing. Subtitles are shit, crud. Hollywood reminds me that anything in translation is mediocre. My red carpet wardrobe: shit, crud. What am I wearing to the snusk shed? No pretty musk, all should snusk closely into my snusk shed. I mosh onward, slashed and dripping riot dye, graffiti. Why am I trying to make sense of this world of graffiti? Why should I bother translating? Suddenly, I hear them. Suddenly, I remember their names. My son's name: Meat-He. My daughter's: Oak-Her.

The ochre branches of the tree of sores pinching up my sleeves, at my filthy body. Tentakler surround, vampyroteuthis. Tooths this, barcode body mine. I suddenly find myself covered in pearlish ulcers and tongues of worship. I become painfully decorated by the tree of heirlooms, the tree of sores. Its meathook branches take hold of me, holes me up ageless, to the light, pushes me into the overneath of the house. Crushes me with commercial light, viral bric-à-brac. Lobes of God, I rock and roll. Stockholm kaffe table, Stockholm glas-door cabinet, Stockholm takkrona. Tentakler, blood-stealing IVs reaching into my retching spaces. I feel like vampyroteuthis, expanding my own Star Queen Nebula. I wake up, anguish, convulsing, in and out of a frame of sublime gaseousness. My black bed, my black sheets of space, my tertius gaudens. My venous sinuses, I receive more than one language. I become feathered, eternal flood of blasphemy. I eat these unknown scraps, this skåp.

"The little girl points to a soft, cephalopodal something on a shelf behind me. I pick it up, I study it, I show it to them, I ask, *Kraken*?" In 2013, crochet octopuses (virkade bläckfisk) were banned from Skåne University Hospital in Malmö due to claims from the medical staff that the plush animals were spreading bacteria and posing a risk of infection to infants. Supposedly the crochet tentacles have been said to be comforting for premature infants because they closely resemble an umbilical cord. The crochet octopuses trend originated in Denmark.

"Bolsonaro dreams of a clean world, dreams of smoke." On August 10, 2019 (also known as Fire Day), farmers from Novo Progresso—in the state of Pará—contributed to the widespread wildfires devastating Amazonian Indigenous lands by setting their properties ablaze in support of President Jair Bolsonaro (a notorious opponent of climate-change). *Foreign Policy* reported that after deploying the Brazilian Armed Forces to the Amazon, the "operation lasted until Oct. 24 and, according to the Defense Ministry, resulted in 127 arrests and more than $33 million in fines." President Donald Trump tweeted: "He is working very hard on the Amazon fires and in all respects doing a great job for the people of Brazil - Not easy. He and his country have the full and complete support of the USA!"

"Clearly I cannot recall my little tree, my kvitto tree, my ancient ek, my traditional ick, my family tree, my bra vibrationer." The phrase, "bra vibrationer" (or "vibes" or "vibrations") is actually the same name of a song by Swedish pop singer, Kikki Danielsson. Danielsson performed "Bra Vibrationer" in the Eurovision Song Contest in 1985.

"Hand-drawn, henjawn." The word, "hen," is a gender-neutral personal pronoun in Swedish. The word, "jawn," is Philadelphia slang for an unspecified person or thing.

THE TREE OF SORES

Fly the eagle
Start all over again
I can't depend on these so-called friends
It's a pity you need to bend
I'll take the furniture
Start all over again.

-Public Image Ltd., "The Flowers of Romance"

My unglued, my unmade hands. My hen coordinates gone awry. My body rolls over a tuft of rattan, stalks of office bamboo. My ball-bearings slide, I am dramatically framed. Blown glass. I take in the surroundings. Fejka office, fejka bamboo. My bearings, my solids, my drawerfronts. My dream always opening, closing. The sun feels surprisingly gentle against my surfaces. *All this light, all this glass! Am I in a furniture store or a greenhouse?* I stand up, I am standing in a room filled with lamps. Thousands of lamps. I squint endlessly. Every last lamp turned On-On-On-On. I look down at my feet, I am standing on a stage inside a strange crystal palace. I look down at my feet, thick roots growing across my shoes. Cable management, I cry tears of sleep. On-Off-On-Off.

Pappa, why are you crying? I try rubbing the bulbs from my eyes. My children rush to my side, hug me tightly. Tightly, the tree of sores snakes around me, its roots congeal against my storefront skin. The tree, its roots covered in sinister, frothing sores—they burn me. *Pappa, why?* But not the way my children once burned me. I stare up into the tree's girth, I experience a rush of memory. The friends I have known during my lifetime. A military scrapheap of bodies, one 21-gun salute too many. Decorated soldiers turned drug addicts. *Pappa?* I imagine I am a swivel chair, constantly turning to face yet another familiar family parlor, yet another familiar scene of early childhood talkings and makings. My eardrömmar hammer with future gunshot after future gunshot. I suddenly see my oldest and my greatest friend, the boy-soldier smothered by the flag of stars and stripes. *In America, you can go far!* You see, something happens between 17 and 18, something happens to a body.

The pulse of lamps, a funeral procession. On-Off-On-Off. You see, something happens to a body between 17 and 18. A cemetery, a tradition. He had his fill, my friend. Bullets, vital organs. I swivel, and I swivel. Room, after room. Gray patterned swivel, tested and approved swivel, clear lacquered birch swivel. Tradition, tradition. I remember the day the soil slowly crept over my friend, I remember the cost. I remember his mother, with the elephant pin, crying onto her smooth oak countertops, her bleka skin, her elephant trunk sniffling. The way she sank into her densely woven bed, satin pillows. *Pappa, why are you crying?*

Furniture is often a poor decision. The many lamps lick my eyes, I feel nauseous. I can't hold back my insides. Flags, banners, regalia. The stuff of patriots. *Pappa, är du sjuk*, Oak-Her asks. *I think so*, I answer in English. Oak-Her produces a toy medical kit. Meat-He produces a dry washcloth and dabs the sweat from my forehead. I touch my Oak-Her's cheek as she presses a plastic stethoscope to my chest. *Är du virklig*, I ask her. Oak-Her stares at me, laughs, and I wish she would never stop that laughing. She sings:

för har du mig kär

but if i know you

förblir du ju här

i know what you'll do

allt blir då med ens

you'll love me at once

det sätt du gjorde en gang

the way you did once

som i en dröm

once upon a dream

Hmmm. You're a bad translator, pappa, says Meat-He. *Translation is a very bad thing*, says Oak-Her. *I'm sorry, I wasn't trying to upset you*, I tell them, feeling sick again. The roots of the tree of sores suddenly swallow them up, takes them into its roots. Red-Blue-Red-Blue. I stare at my half-swallowed mediocre son, I stare at my half-swallowed mediocre daughter. I finally think I am living the American Dream. Am I? Did we look like a Swedish family? Or an all-American family? Maybe I am American after all? Me, my son, my daughter. We had good times, we had hardships. Red-Blue-Red-Blue. I stare at my family tree of rifles and ammunition. Reflections of the real. He was 18 years old. We went to high school together. My boss tells me to *shut up* whenever I mention the deceased boy-soldier. *He wasn't a boy, he was a man. He was a man who died for his country. You should be proud of him.*

I pull my Swedish children out of the hungry tree, I pull them away from their reflections, the windows. I put them into a yellow bag. I won't let the mirrors have them.

Somewhere in the tree of sores, I kan hear America. Bullet-wounded. Somewhere in the tree of sores, I can hear Europe. Bullet-wounded. This tree has been leaking into me like infection, whispering with inflections I do not recognize. Wounds or words. In what direction am I looking? I no longer know what language I speak. I cannot pin down this tree. I no longer know where my family tree grows. I have lost my roots. I am waiting for the judges to say something. *Dom. Död. Död. Död. Dom. Död. Död. Död*

I am waiting for the judges to say something about my performance. I am standing on a stage inside a crystal palace. I cannot make out the audience. Their faces look like television snow. Too many lights, too many sores. Meat-He and Oak-Her join me for a moment. Oak-Her hands me her microphone, Meat-He wraps a gentleman's cape around my torso. Oak-Her glues a tiny square of mustache to my upper lip, Meat-He places a solid black bowler on top of my head. Oak-Her says, *You're going to be a finalist, I just know it*. Meat-He says, *Make us proud, pappa!*

I see myself reflected in the windows of the crystal palace. The reflection looks like Charlie Chaplin or Adolf Hitler. A homeless woman wanders out of the crowd, wanders onto the stage, approaches the judges. *You bulldozed my family for a crystal palace*, she screams. *My children are homeless*, she weeps. *I am homeless!* The judges call security and security removes the homeless woman. The judges call my name and I take the stage. There are strobe lights, there are lasers. I hear insidious music. *Dom. Död. Död. Död. Dom. Död. Död. Död.*

"Dream Empire" (a song to be sung in an inspiring way)

Why, why was I assigned to this dangerous task?
Today, I worry there's something that I lack.
Am I your American cool, American fool?
Oh, oh, why do I believe in, why do I believe in…

Dreeeeeam Empiiiire
Are you in me?
Are you just my imagination?
I'm turning on-off-on-off-on-off-on-off
Dreeeeeam Empiiiire
Is my sense of pride on fire?
Can I toast to victory?
I'm turning on-off-on-off-on-off-on-off

Here I am, alone
Oh, here I am, alone, where does a body belong?
Why so forever, why this life so long?
I'm reaching, turning on-off-on-off-on-off.

Dreeeeeam Empiiiire
Why, why was I assigned to this dangerous task?
Today, I worry there's something I lack.
I'm turning on-off-on-off-on-off-on-off
Dreeeeeam Empiiiire
Is my sense of pride on fire?
Can I toast to victory?
I'm turning on-off-on-off-on-off-on-off

America, are you as miraculous as the voices say?
Can I, can I toast to victory?

Dreeeeeam Empiiiire
I'm turning on-off-on-off-on-off-on-off
Dreeeeeam Empiiiire
Is my sense of pride on fire?
Can I toast to victory?
I'm turning on-off-on-off-on-off-on-off
on-off-on-off-on-off
on-off-on-off-on-off-on-off-on-off

Judge's Comments:

I'm going to have to say no. It's a resounding no for me. A no-brainer, in fact. Are you under the weather? Where and tearing? You were shockingly bad.

Yeah, it was just mediocre, really. No charisma, no talent. Diabolical. Diluted vibrato. It felt very foreign to me. I couldn't listen to another minute of it. It was excruciatingly bad.

Right. I genuinely disliked the performance. Your delivery was ridiculous. You have no star-quality, zero flare. Everything was wrong. The stage just isn't for everybody. Have you looked in a mirror lately?

on-off-on-off-on-off-on-off-on-off-on-off-on-off-on-off-on-off-
on-off-on-off-on-off-on-off-on-off-on-off-on-off-on-off-on-off-
on-off-on-off-on-off-on-off-on-off-on-off-on-off-on-off-on-off-
on-off-on-off-on-off-on-off-on-off-on-off-on-off-on-off-on-off-
on-off-on-off-on-off-on-off-on-off-on-off-on-off-on-off-on-off-
on-off-on-off-on-off-on-off-on-off-on-off-on-off-on-off-on-off-
on-off-on-off-on-off-on-off-on-off-on-off-on-off-on-off-on-off-
on-off-on-off-on-off-on-off-on-off-on-off-on-off-on-off-on-off-
on-off-on-off-on-off-on-off-on-off-on-off-on-off-on-off-on-off-
on-off-on-off-on-off-on-off-on-off-on-off-on-off-on-off-on-off-
on-off-on-off-on-off-on-off-on-off-on-off-on-off-on-off-on-off-
on-off-on-off-on-off-on-off-on-off-on-off-on-off-on-off-on-off-
on-off-on-off-on-off-on-off-on-off-on-off-on-off-on-off-on-off-
on-off-on-off-on-off-on-off-on-off-on-off-on-off-on-off-on-off-

I wake up inside a large room, a bord room. Board by board, bord by bord, border after bordar. From the Grand Foyer, I survey the Bord Room. Two staircases, everything plain, wooden. Plain wooden walls, plain wooden floors. Floor boards shift and slide out from under my feet. I lose my balance, collapse onto the up-down of the piano teeth floor. Carved panels of dull tulips, wooden doves cooing, wooden slats sliding into grooves of wood. Bowing mahogany biceps of wood. Wide splays of mahoganized American businessmen projecting onto me with their bullseyes, horizontal turnings on the bord floor. My final position, my measly flitches of human attached to cutting bord. From the Grand Foyer, the mahoganized ones insert their screws through my top and bottom bracket holes. Daddy is mahoganized now, Uncle Sam'd. I am shellacked with smooth terminals. I am a bed, I am sliding into final position. A tuckaway, a *shhhhhhh*...

I am seated on the bord room floor of dyed would, heavily dyed would, dyed with knuckle-blood, long zigzags of black cherried birch. I am seated between two young soldier-corpses, *What wood they have been*, I wonder. I smell family smokestack smoke, I smell family fuel burnt up. Evidence of worms, of termites. Evidence of glory. I think of the word, glory. Grubs of glory. *Inte gråta över spilld mjölk,* I tell myself. *No*, I tell myself. I have to remember to use the language I was born into. But how can I escape the surveillance of this world if I am not everywhere? *No crying over spilled milk*, I ask. *What about blood*, I ask. *What about glory.* The termites pull me into plain view, the maggots sing from inside the soldiers, the votes shall them be counted. The hour of glory, your-glory, his-glory. History. It is not votes, it is but safety warnings. I do solemnly swear.

Bored of personal glory, the centermost bord room table lures me into its roundabout proper. I desire a strong drink. It is 4 AM and I am. I am, after all. I shall act accordingly, and fix myself a strong drink. But I am caught, cape-caught-on-table caught. Two-thirds of the senators present wood concur: I am caught, attached to bord after board. I spin with the tabletop, I circle the same floorboards. Eventually I tear myself away from the table, from the fidelity of the word. I fall back, into the woodpile, into congressional consent, the deathly police-interior of walnut veneered bonnet-tops and bottoms, cusped edges of rocket's red flame finials, a pornography of pointed knees, yours, mine. Cyma curves, cyma-cut edging. Moaning, professional editing. A surround of compartments, uniform departments, paneled doors. "In Police we trust!" I walk across the plain wooden floor, carry my torn away self from the cape, carry my torn away cape to the wooden corner coat rack. It refuses my cape, its serpentine front tentacles to and fro. It slowly hardens into a tree branch of leafy oval eagle brasses. I stare into a history of satanwood, "In Police we trust!"

Meat-He and Oak-Her run past, push me down. They take the arm of the banister, rush quickly to the top of the Grand Foyer. They look frightened, rashy, like narrow wooden strips of red. *My children*, I cry, *Why are you running from me?* My son screams, *I am a fall hazard.* My daughter screams, *I am a strangulation hazard.* I chase after them, I ascend the stairs. Above and below, the wooden bordar splitting and hissing. Thickly swirling vase-pillars of wood, drum-headed spindles of wood. They snake across my field of vision, push me hard. I Charlie Chaplin down the stairs, become a tangle of thorns and branches, nuts and screws. I grip the nearby banister tightly until, it too, swells grotesquely into a branch of thorns. Strands of shredding, masses of suborbital veins plumping into thorns. I cannot hold on, I slide down the banister-branch. My soft palms, palmette-carved. Wounds, sores—*everywhere*. Inlaid stars, fluted stripes.

One of the tree's tentacles whip me hard, lifts me onto the centermost table. I am spinning again, running in place. A spinning, burning earth suspended in a house of mirrors. A humiliated earth. A burdened body, running in place atop the eagle'd globes of plinths, of withering root systems. Bord systems. I punch at the air with my bloody fists—left, right, left, right. I run in place, my carved up hands rain red yolks across the table, my ground-up knuckles, my heavy avgrund shavings infect the Grand Foyer. I leap from my red table to a tea table. (Blood spills.) I leap from the tea table to a sideboard of striated mahogany. (Canon fire.) I leap from the sideboard to a card table. (*Enough gambling.*) I step down, I stand below storage shelves, cupboardspaces and openwork hearts. I am framed by wooden swags of fruit, rosettes, flames. I become gadrooned, double-screwed. I am somewhere beneath the peel, somewhere *before* the burning fruit. America.

I don't want to be a goner in this pentagonal interior, this cabin of wood, this cabinet of moulded shafts. The staircases of the Grand Foyer, still blocked by bulbous thorn inlays, jagged rifles, intersecting lunettes. I drift across the horrifying floor, dodge the hologram arrows. I dodge protruding wooden pegs, dangerous bellflowers, corkscrew finials. Again, I approach the corner coatrack, I climb its ladder, on the right track, its cuffs of rosewood, its woundwould. I scale the Grand Foyer, I drip from its swans. No sign of Meat-He or Oak-Her, only a circular face painted in sun and moon. Time, waiting to pulverize me. Furniture, waiting to corpse.

Box-on-box mahogany, a mechanic assemblage, a column of clock aims its leafy pendulum at my body. Then comes the family heirlooms, the tree of sores: claw-and-ball feet and gate-legged tables; cushion-footed beasts of fine craftsmanship. Their wooden holes flaring. A chest of drawers manhandles me, a smack, a wing chair to my sternum. I pinch at my face, I slap at my face. I forget about my bleeding hands, I forget about myself. More importantly, no glasses. I desperately stick a finger into my eye, I cry out. No glasses, no Instruction Manual! No awakening, no dreaming. My senses, neutralized. *Where am I?* Hemorrhaging herringbone bands pulverize my torso, claw marks across my face. I feel infected, deterritorialized.

4 AM feels long ago, my body the peeled away orange. The ceiling leaks swags of pus-fruit, citrus scent. A shiny panel slides across a nearby wall. In the reflection of the wood, I see my son. Meat-He, reflected back at me. I feel finished off by his mirror. His meat-sheen. Adult no more, I am boy uttering prayer-like lines of escape, over and over…

Carve my name on this tree, a future page in a book. Remember that I was once Dada Rotten. I once opened my mouth in protest! Ruttna microphone warning of rotten police. Ideology and manipulation. RASVÄRLD! SORGVÄRLD! Rage-world, sorrow-world of repressive apparatuses, a song of sorg, my tree of sores! In the next world, the world to come, all is reckoning! Räknar allt! The fires of purification! Play music loudly, for it is blasphemy! Sing poetry loudly, for it is blasphemy! Do not read news articles, do not pay for subscriptions, do not conduct interviews, do not retweet, do not believe in presidents! Just embrace kaos. Americans love violence more than art. Americans need guns more than art. Why educate when you can shooting range? Amerikaner älskar vapen! Americans are vipers. They inject, inject, inject! With poison fangs. Gone as far as they can go – gift! Poison! Gift! Tillbaka till kaos, tillbaka till kaos...

Squealing, the openwork hands of the clock wind rapidly. It spews golden scrollwork from an opening in its gilt paterae, its drawers—sliding out rapidly! Out and in, out and in! Bolts and screws flailing! They stamp welts into my arms, my chest. I back away from the wooden beasts, I follow the golden tongue to a wall of loose wooden panels. I peel away the weak wood, I discover a hallway. *A secret passageway? An exit? A varning?* I hallar into the long-haul. No answer. The wooden beasts persist. I persist until unseeable. Until I am too late.

I travel the length of the hallway, a candlelit room in the distance. I enter the empty candlelit room, the light flickers across the wooden interior. Four walls, a ceiling, a floor. All six faces of a cubic interior: interchangeable. All but one. One wall containing a window rests directly in front of me. The window, a single pane of glass, is all that separates me from the outside sky. The outside resembles something not quite night, not quite day. I feel as though I am looking through the window of a space station. Only there are no stars, no sun, no children, no earth. I stand in a cabin floating in starless space. I stand on floor, or ceiling. I stare at night, or day. I let my forehead knock-knock-knock against the cold of the window. The knock-knock-knock makes a hairline crack. My hemoglobin roots itself into the crack of the glass, the wound. My reflection distorted. The hemoglobin shed from my forehead shivers, throbs against the cold of the unrecognizable outside. It spreads somehow, across the glass. Like paint. It willows—sticky ribbons of red. I pick up the candle, hold it to the window.

Gluish geodes burst from the mutating blood tract, chains of miniature tendons knotting into mounds of new, hairless flesh. The glass fogs over, tiny red capillary branches sway side-to-side outside the window. Tiny branches gel and smear, the branches tirelessly sculpt and twist into the heavy silk of a facial frame. My hemoglobin produces predetermined content, pushes matter away from the cabin where I will most likely remain. I stand behind myself, a painful sensation spreads through my lower back, my kidneys fail. My muscles lose their hoist, my eyelids dissolve. I experience debilitating contractions. A pendulum hammers my vital organs, hammers my spandrels of human into ruins. My spine, my *I*—slurped up clock. Lantern dimming, nervous system dimming.

America, a *nervous* system. The window, bronzed with new meat, grows a new system, protrudes into serpentine arms and intricate threads of marrow. I stare into the future: combat. A new solider of language. I stare into the cavernous halves of new organs suction cupping the window for dear life. Yet another new body that doesn't have a chance. The next body, my outside body, it writhes, it writes words all over the glass. *Will I be standing on the other side of my human when the window shatters?* What will the Imaginary Swedes think? No one answers. I cannot imagine. My little wooden room of war and milk will leak into an inaccessible domain, a poem. An infinite field of eggs. A space station of signals lost. I cannot assist, I cannot manage…

…on-off-on-off…

"*You bulldozed my family for a crystal palace*, she screams."
In 2012, Azerbaijan officials evicted nearly 300 families from their homes to make room for the construction of the Eurovision Song Contest's Crystal Hall. An Azerbaijani group (called Bulistan) responded by writing a song called "Vermisel." The lyrics: "My house is demolished / I'm homeless / No roof over my head / Is Eurovision what I need now? / Cameras are all over the place / Someone is watching us / Here is the message to them: Saint middle finger."

Source: *Empire of Song: Europe and Nation in the Eurovision Song Contest* (Rowman & Littlefield, Scarecrow Press, Inc, 2013)

ACKNOWLEDGMENTS

Grateful thanks to the editors of the following literary journals who published earlier versions of some of these poems for the first time: *Bat City Review*; *Ghost Proposal*; *OmniVerse*; *Real Pants*; *SAND: Berlin's English Literary Journal*; *Hound*; *Seven Corners*; *Spork*; *TAGVVERK*; *Toad Suck Review*; and *Yalobusha Review*.

Endless thanks to Gary J. Shipley for publishing this interlingual book of dark dreams.

A very special thank you to Johannes Göransson and Joyelle McSweeney for your generous suggestions, reading recommendations, and engagement with this manuscript.

Thanks to my friend and past collaborator Sam Shoemaker for giving my first book its antlers.

Thanks to Barry McCrea and Maria DiBattista for inviting me into INCH. Deborah Nord, Helena Buescu, Rafael Esteves Martins, Amândio Reis, Simona Micali, Beth Guilding, Jill Wharton, Sara Di Simone, Valleria Cavalloro, Nicole Winsor, Beatrice Mazzi, Julien Zanetta, Eva Kenny, Rae Gaubinger, Oliver Browne, Orlando Reade, Kate Clairmont, Jen Minnen, Brian Gingrich, Moeko Fujii, and others—thank you for your friendship and support!

Thanks to the friends, mentors, and artists who, if even in some small way, have undeniably supported or contributed to who and where I am today: Claudia Fath, Atom Atkinson, Jake

Syersak, Quentin Panger, Karter Schachner, Madeline Weiss, Gia Fagnelli, Milan Ginocchi, Ryan Janusko, Nick Hannan, Aase Berg, Sade LaNay, Don Mee Choi, Valerie Mejer-Caso, Katherine M. Hedeen, Olivia Lott, Kim Koga, Sawako Nakayasu, Ronaldo Wilson, Michael Mejia, Dennis Cooper, Rauan Klassnik, Derek White, DA Powell, Blake Butler, Steve Tomasula, Roy Scranton, Sarah E. Brook, Pete Figler, Danette DiMarco, Mark O'Connor, Rachela Permenter, William Covey, Derek Pitard, Joseph McCarren, Steve Halle, Magdalena Zurawski, CAConrad, Andrew Zawacki, LeAnne Howe, Richard Menke, Esra Santesso, Steve Halle, Danielle Susi-Dittmore, Rusty Morrison, Myung Mi Kim, Adam Robinson, Richard Siken, Robert Meehan, Barrett White, Marty Cain, Maggie Woodward, Jeffrey Lance, Andrew Dally, Rachel Zavecz, Jace Brittain, Dev Varma, Peter Twal, Chris Holdaway, Sarah Roth, Jayme Russell, Nichole Goff, Coleen Hoover, Ed Steck, Greg Nissan, Sam Regal, Claire Cronin, Madison McCartha, Matt Kliewer, Christian Gallichio, Renee Buesking, Danielle Gilman, Paula Rawlins, Kensie Poor, Amy Bonnaffons, Zack Anderson, and Nathan Dixon.

My deepest gratitude to my family: Ed, Nora, and Brandon.

Paul Cunningham is from Pittsburgh, PA. From the Swedish, he is the translator of Helena Österlund's *Words* (OOMPH! Press, 2019). He has also translated two chapbooks by Sara Tuss Efrik: *Automanias: Selected Poems* (Goodmorning Menagerie, 2016) and *The Night's Belly* (Toad Press, 2016). His creative and critical work has appeared in *Poem-a-Day*, *7x7.la*, *Kenyon Review*, *Quarterly West*, *Harvard Review*, *DIAGRAM*, *OmniVerse*, *Bat City Review*, and others. His latest chapbook of poetry is *The Inmost* (Carrion Bloom Books, 2020). He is an Associate Editor of Action Books, co-editor of *Deluge*, co-managing editor of Radioactive Cloud, and co-founder of the Yumfactory Reading Series. Cunningham is an invited member of the International Network of Comparative Humanities, funded by Princeton University and the University of Notre Dame. He is a PhD candidate at the University of Georgia, and he holds an MFA in Poetry from the University of Notre Dame.

SCHISM²